MACHINES ON THE MOVE

TOW TRUCKS

by Natalie Deniston

TABLE OF CONTENTS

Words to Know 2

Pull 3

Let's Review! 16

Index 16

WORDS TO KNOW

bed

hook

pulls

stuck

tows

truck

PULL

A car is stuck.

A tow truck comes!

It has a hook.

It goes on the car.

It pulls the car out!

bed

This one has a bed.

A car is on it.

This one tows big trucks.

LET'S REVIEW!

Tow trucks tow cars. This means they move them. What part of a tow truck is this?

INDEX

bed 12
car 3, 9, 11, 13
hook 7
pulls 11
tows 14
trucks 14